Welcome to the EVERYDAY POSITIVITY Workbook

with Kate Cocker

Hello and welcome to the first Everyday Positivity Workbook. I am so excited to share this with you!

Everyday Positivity is a movement to encourage people to keep a positive mindset every day. It started out in 2018 as a daily podcast that I intended to be a reminder to be kind to yourself. Now we have created a community that supports its members and spreads positivity around the world... and we have a lot of fun too. (Come and find us in the facebook group "Everyday Positivity with Kate Cocker" if you haven't already).

What I know to be true is that we live in a world where we have got into the habit of judgement, blame, shame and negativity, and that we have to work at creating a positive and growth mindset. That means we have to do that daily. Little by little. Step by step. And so this workbook is born.

It's essentially a colouring book so you can create time and space to focus your attention and be mindful (one of the Pillars Of Positivity that you will find out about in this book). And my lovely team have designed this and added some extras in for you - meditations and quotes.

Don't forget to listen to the podcast too - search Everyday Positivity wherever you get your podcasts.

I really hope you enjoy this book - and remember - you have 100% got this :)

Kate x

Statement of Intent

I am committed to cultivating a positive and growth mindset by taking care of me.

I set the intention
to care for myself,
to heal myself,
to accept myself,
to love myself.

I set the intention
to be grateful for what I have,
to live courageously,
to manage my energy,
And to do the work that means that I can thrive.

I love myself. I love myself. I love myself.

Signed: _____

Date: _____

THE 7 PILLARS OF POSITIVITY

Research shows that our brains are wired to have a negative bias. It's supposed to be there! Our negative bias allows us to protect ourselves in times of strife. The thing is that when we try to run our lives from this place, it can become a struggle. So we have to work at positivity - and I truly believe that positivity is a skill.

Now let me be clear - when I talk about positivity I don't mean that we pretend everything is OK when it isn't. Some people might call that "toxic" positivity.

For me positivity is not about pasting a smile over the cracks of life. Positivity IS about knowing that you have all you need to cope with the cracks of life

With this in mind I devised the 7 Pillars of Positivity as things to practice regularly and to draw upon when things feel sticky.

PILLAR 1
BE SELFUL

PILLAR 2
ACCEPT THE NOW

PILLAR 3
PRACTICE GRATITUDE

PILLAR 4
CHECK YOUR SELF TALK

PILLAR 5
MAKE RAINBOWS

PILLAR 6
REST, RECOUP, RECHARGE, SLEEP

PILLAR 7
CLEAR YOUR MIND

"POSITIVITY IS NOT ABOUT PASTING A SMILE OVER THE CRACKS OF LIFE...

... IT'S ABOUT KNOWING THAT YOU CAN COPE WITH THE CRACKS OF LIFE."

KATE COCKER

EVERYDAY POSITIVITY

EVERYDAY POSITIVITY

BREATH MEDITATION FOR CALMNESS

Get yourself into a comfortable position away from distractions.

Get your feet level on the floor and feel the floor come back at you, even if you are sitting.

Relax your shoulders - imagine your shoulder blades have weights on them and they are being pulled towards the floor.

Inhale.

Exhale.

Continue breathing naturally, feel the air enter through your nostrils, then exit through your nostrils. Continue to feel your breath.

Do this until you feel comfortable with a deep breath.

Then, on the inhale really focus on bringing the air into your belly. Aim for the bottom of your lungs. And be aware of the breath coming in.

On the exhale, let the breath fully out, this time through your mouth, till you can't get any more air out.

Pause for a second

And inhale through your nose again.

Continue with this breath, feeling the depth of the breath. Let it move in through your nose, throat, chest and belly. Then back out through your belly, chest, throat and mouth.

Repeat this for a while - and let the breath take you to where you need to go. Allow your mind to focus on the breath.

Begin to feel the breath as a wave coming up from the belly and rising to the top of the breath beneath the throat.

Continue with this wave-like breath, rolling in and up, hold it for two seconds, and then roll back out like a tide.

Feel the fluidity of the breath. Feel the complete cycle of the breath. Focus only on the breath.

Finish a final cycle of this breath and after the complete exhale, return to your natural breath.

Feel the steadiness of your breath.

Feel the ease.

Feel the calmness.

JOURNALING PROMPTS

On this page there are six journaling prompts for you to respond to and help you think about positive parts of your life that bring you joy and happiness. The prompts are designed to help you reflect, and just write write write. This is part of Pillar of Positivity Number 7 - clear your mind.

3 THOUGHTS THAT MAKE ME SMILE

o _____
_____
_____

o _____
_____
_____

o _____
_____
_____

3 THINGS THAT HAVE CHALLENGED ME

o _____
_____
_____

o _____
_____
_____

o _____
_____
_____

3 PRODUCTIVE TASKS I'VE DONE

o _____
_____
_____

o _____
_____
_____

o _____
_____
_____

3 ACTIONS THAT MADE ME FEEL LOVED

o _____
_____
_____

o _____
_____
_____

o _____
_____
_____

3 BEAUTIFUL THINGS I'VE HEARD

o _____
_____
_____

o _____
_____
_____

o _____
_____
_____

3 BEAUTIFUL THINGS I'VE SEEN

o _____
_____
_____

o _____
_____
_____

o _____
_____
_____

GRATITIUDE JOURNAL

Gratitude is the lever by which we pull ourselves out of a funk.

People who regularly practice gratitude by reflecting on the parts of their lives they are thankful for experience more positive emotions, feel more alive, sleep better and express more compassion and kindness.

Use this page as a gratitude journal, take some time to come here and write down a few things that you are thankful for in your life, they can be as small as a refreshing, icy can of coke with your dinner or as big as a loving family that supports you.

GRATITUDE MEDITATION

Get yourself into a comfortable position away from distractions.

Take a minute to focus on your breath, relax your body, clear your mind.

Once you are settled into your breath, let your thoughts rest and settle down. Clear your mind and begin to focus on this question…

What has got me here today that I am grateful for?

You can start literally - what got you here? What type of transport are you grateful for? What got you that transport?

Then you might want to think about the people in your life who are special:
Who got you here? How did they support you?
Who are the people in your life that are the gifts that support you?

Think about all the people you know that have been there, that means that you have arrived at this point in your life? Who are your champions? Who makes you smile?

Maybe there are pets you are grateful for too?

Now think about yourself, reasons you are grateful for being you, what self-care do you or could you offer yourself in the same way that these people that you know, and some that you don't, support you.

Take some time to experience this feeling of gratitude for things you have had in the past, what you have now and what you may have in the future. Stretch your hands and your arms, your feet and your legs.

Go to the gratitude journal page and note down some of the things that you have felt grateful for during this meditation.

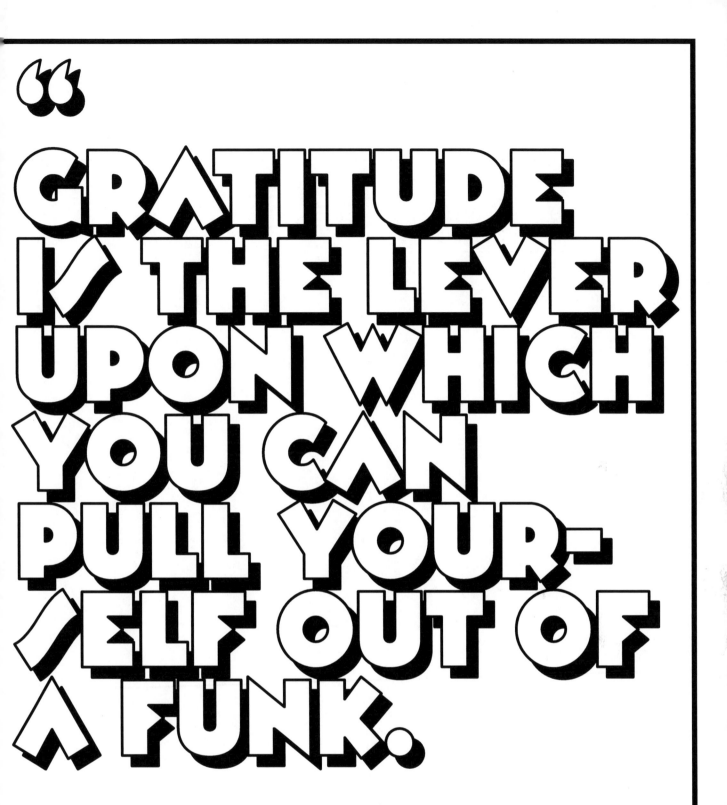

"GRATITUDE IS THE LEVER UPON WHICH YOU CAN PULL YOUR-SELF OUT OF A FUNK."

KATE COCKER

REFLECTION JOURNAL

On this page take some time to reflect on everything that has happened recently in your life, note down some achievements that make you feel proud, changes in your life that have had a positive effect on you and lessons you have learnt that you want to take forward with you through life.

ACHIEVEMENTS I AM PROUD OF

POSITIVE CHANGES I'VE EXPERIENCED

LESSONS I HAVE LEARNT

WHAT IS YOUR MANTRA?

Use this page to illustrate your own mantra or quote, it could be from someone who inspires you or something you have come up with yourself. A mantra is a word or set of words that are often used in Hindu and Buddist meditation practices but can be used at any time to help ground yourself when feeling anxious or low.

Find a phrase that brings you comfort and helps you to reach a positive head space when you repeat it to yourself.

You could simply write it out, use paints and colouring pencils, or cut up letters from a magazine or newspaper and stick them down - do whatever makes most sense to you.

SMILE MEDITATION

Get yourself into a comfortable position away from distractions.

Relax and focus on your breath - inhale and exhale at a gentle pace till you feel comfortable and relaxed.

When you are relaxed… Smile.

Bring a big grin to your face, let it stretch from ear to ear.

Feel the warmth of that smile in your face and focus on how good the smile feels.

Let the warmth of the smile travel down your neck, into your shoulders, and down your arms. Feel the warmth.

Let it go into your heart and your belly. Let the warmth sit well in your belly, and feel it glow, and grow.

Then the smile can act like a wave that washes through your legs and right down to your toes. You can still have a smile on your face.

Now your whole body should feel full of the warmth of a smile - and you can really focus on the warmth in your centre.

Focus on the smile in your chest and belly, and let it heat up like a ball of light. Allow that light to glow, and grow.

Glow and grow.

Glow and grow.

And feel that smile on your face get warmer and warmer.

Let the light shine bright in you. And let the light escape from you too - the beam of your smile radiating through your body and out of your skin.

And as you are aware of that warmth and the glow, and the growth of that warmth, then bring your breath back into focus.

Keep smiling, keep breathing and own the warmth of the smile.

Feel the warmth, feel the joy and take it with you into the world.

SELF-CARE GOALS

Self-care is vital to maintaining your mental health so on this page plan out a few goals that you'd like to achieve that are just for you - this could be learning a new skill or putting some time aside to pamper yourself, maybe a bath, some chocolate and a book.

Give yourself a measurable goal and then break it down into small achievable steps that you can follow to reach your aim.

GOAL _____ **STEPS** _____
- ⭘ _____
  _____
- ⭘ _____
  _____
- ⭘ _____
  _____

GOAL _____ **STEPS** _____
- ⭘ _____
  _____
- ⭘ _____
  _____
- ⭘ _____
  _____

GOAL _____ **STEPS** _____
- ⭘ _____
  _____
- ⭘ _____
  _____
- ⭘ _____
  _____

GOAL _____ **STEPS** _____
- ⭘ _____
  _____
- ⭘ _____
  _____
- ⭘ _____
  _____

GOAL _____ **STEPS** _____
- ⭘ _____
  _____
- ⭘ _____
  _____
- ⭘ _____
  _____

GOAL _____ **STEPS** _____
- ⭘ _____
  _____
- ⭘ _____
  _____
- ⭘ _____
  _____

BUCKET LIST

Use this page to make a note of books, films, tv shows, food, and general experiences that you've been meaning to get around to and tick them off as you go.

BOOKS I WANT TO READ

- ○ ☐
- ○ ☐
- ○ ☐
- ○ ☐
- ○ ☐

TV SHOWS I WANT TO BINGE

- ○ ☐
- ○ ☐
- ○ ☐
- ○ ☐
- ○ ☐

FILMS I WANT TO WATCH

- ○ ☐
- ○ ☐
- ○ ☐
- ○ ☐
- ○ ☐

PODCASTS I WANT TO LISTEN TO

- ○ ☐
- ○ ☐
- ○ ☐
- ○ ☐
- ○ ☐

PLACES I WANT TO VISIT

- ○ ☐
- ○ ☐
- ○ ☐
- ○ ☐
- ○ ☐

FOOD I WANT TO EAT

- ○ ☐
- ○ ☐
- ○ ☐
- ○ ☐
- ○ ☐

PROJECTS I WANT TO START

- ○ ☐
- ○ ☐
- ○ ☐
- ○ ☐
- ○ ☐

EXPERIENCES I WANT TO HAVE

- ○ ☐
- ○ ☐
- ○ ☐
- ○ ☐
- ○ ☐

WE CANNOT CHANGE ANYTHING UNTIL WE ACCEPT IT.

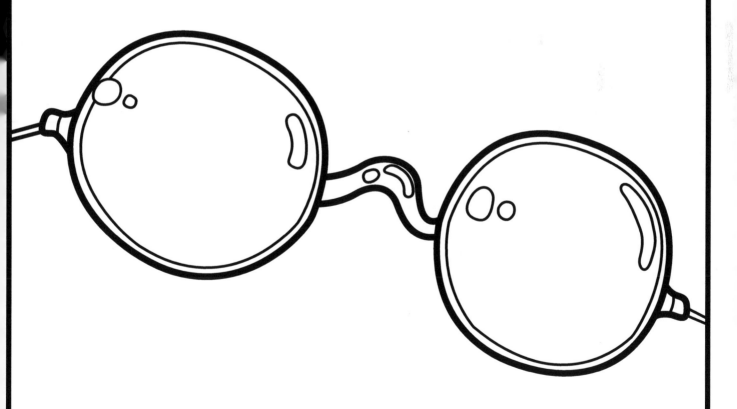

carl jung

WHEEL OF LIFE

This is the Wheel of Life. It is a circle divided into 8 different areas of life which all work together to form our day to day experience.

Use this wheel to assess how satisfied you are with your current situation in each of the areas. This will help you to identify which parts of your life you want to improve on and which parts you are really happy with - you can use this information to help you set goals for how you might begin to improve your day to day living.

Plot a coloured dot for each of the areas starting from 0 (not satisfied) to 10 (completely satisfied) to mark your feelings towards each. Come back in several weeks time and use a different colour to plot how you feel and see if anything has changed.

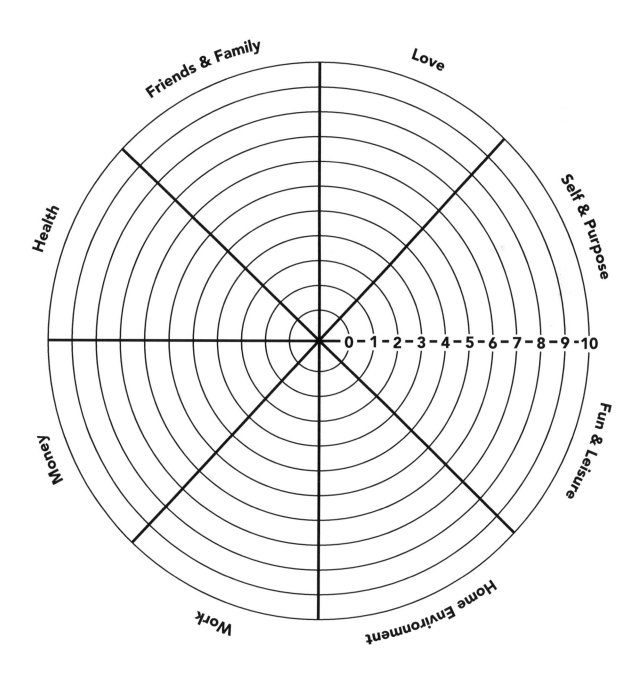

DON'T BE AFRAID TO BE RUBBISH

kate cocker

WHAT IS MEANT FOR YOU WILL NOT PASS YOU BY

proverb

Thank You

By just reading through this book you have taken steps towards creating a positive mindset, and showing yourself that your soul matters. If you have filled in any of the pages then you show your commitment to yourself.

Today you have said "yes" to yourself and that is powerful. When you care for yourself in meaningful ways then you can be the best person for the people you love.

Thank you so much for bringing this book, and Everyday Positivity into your life. I hope this to be the first of many.

Thank you especially to my producer Will Dell for keeping the podcast going always, the team at Volley Inc. Gaby and Riyadh for supporting me from day one and to Elliot Nightingale who has done an exceptional job on the design of this book.

You have 100% got this xx

SCAN THE QR CODE TO LISTEN TO EVERYDAY POSITIVITY NOW!

Words by Kate Cocker. Artwork by Elliot Nightingale.

Printed in Great Britain
by Amazon

12902068R00018